GOD'S CREATION

Adapted by Tess Fries
Illustrated by Cheryl Mendenhall

GOD'S CREATION
Copyright © 2004 Spirit Press,
an imprint of Dalmatian Press, LLC.
All rights reserved

Art Directed by Shannon Osborne Thompson

SPIRIT PRESS and DALMATIAN PRESS are trademarks of
Dalmatian Press, LLC, Franklin, Tennessee 37067.
No part of this book may be reproduced or copied in any form
without the written permission of Dalmatian Press.

ISBN: 1-40370-962-9
11453-0804

Printed in the U.S.A.

04 05 06 07 LBM 10 9 8 7 6 5 4 3 2 1

Long, long ago
the world was
very different
than it is now.
In fact, the world
did not exist at all!
There was only
dark, empty space.
But God was in
the darkness, and
He had a
plan to make
something good.

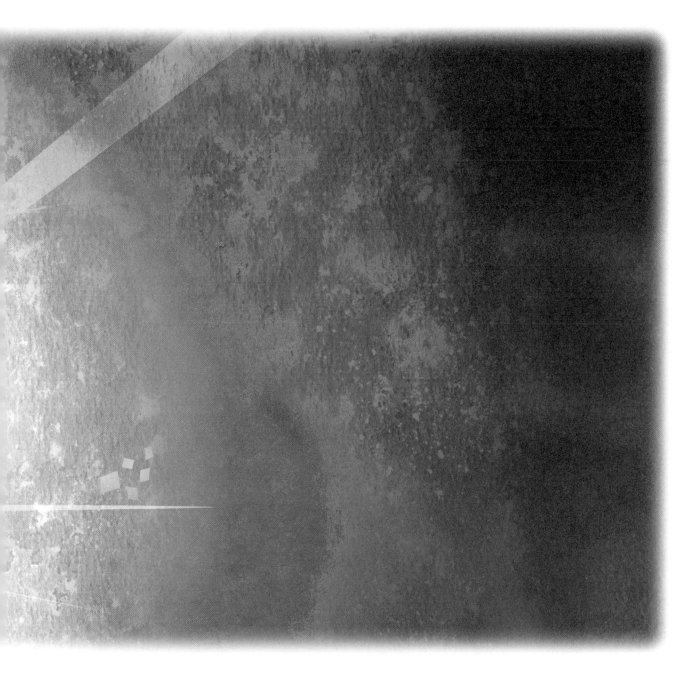

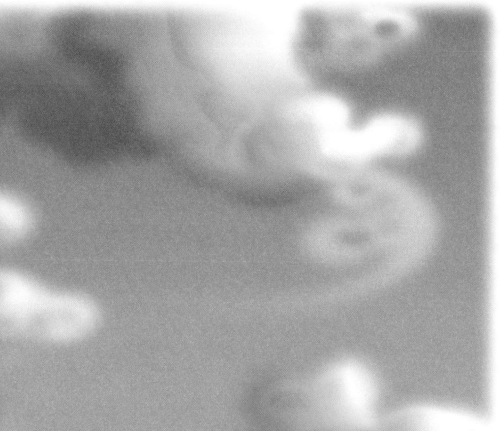

God said "Let there be light," and a golden light shone everywhere. He called the light day and the dark night. This was the very first day.

On the second day, God made the beautiful blue sky. He created the clouds to hold the raindrops.

On the third day, God made the sparkling water and formed the seas and rivers.

He shaped the great mountains and the sloping valleys from the land, then sprinkled the deserts with sand. He planted the fields with tall grasses, trees and colorful flowers. At the end of the third day, God saw that it was good.

God put lights in
the sky on the
fourth day.
He made the
brilliant sun for the
daytime and the
gentle light of the
moon for the night.
He placed each star
in just the right spot
and made them
twinkle and shine.

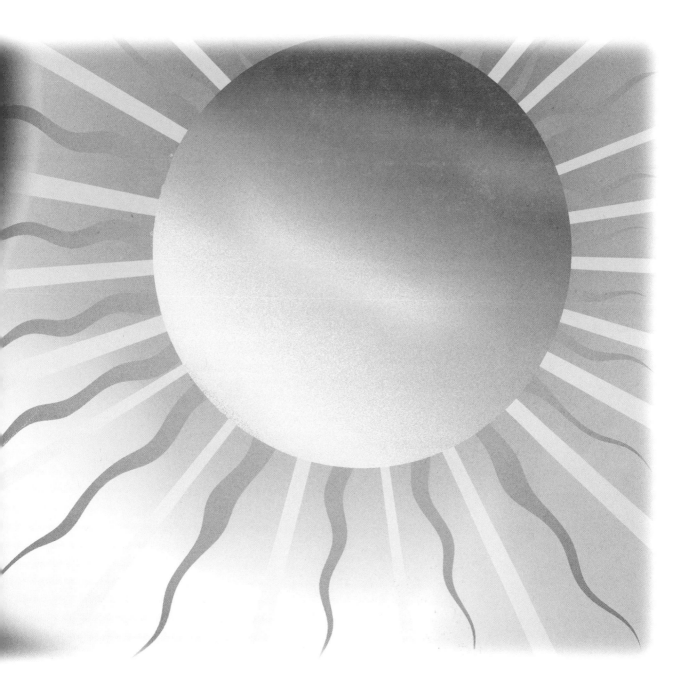

On the fifth day, God made the gigantic whales and the slithering eels. He made the sharks and octopus and every kind of fish to fill the waters.

God also made the birds to sail on the wind and fly through the sky. He made the mighty eagles, the honking geese and the tiny hummingbirds.

On the sixth day, God made all of the animals. He made some with antlers and some with pouches. He created animals that galloped, hopped, roared, growled and mooed.

God wanted someone to rule over the earth and to enjoy His creation. So on the sixth day, God also made the first man. He made him from the dust of the earth and breathed into him, the breath of life. God named him Adam.

On the seventh day, God rested. He saw everything He made, and He knew that it was good.

God is the maker of all things. There will never be anyone greater or more powerful than He is.

God made you just the way you are. He wants you to enjoy His creations and to love Him, for He knows that this is good.

"God saw all that he had made,
and it was very good."
Genesis 1:31
(NIV)